CONCERT FAVORITES

Volume 1

Band Arrangements Correlated with Essential Elements Band Method Book 1

ISBN 978-0-634-05208-8

HAL•LEONARD®

7777 W. BLUEMOUND RD. P.O. BOX 13819 MILWAUKEE, WI 53213

00860128

2

LET'S ROCK!

B♭ TRUMPET

MICHAEL SWEENEY (ASCAP

MAJESTIC MARCH

B♭ TRUMPET

By PAUL LAVENDER

00860128

MICKEY MOUSE MARCH
(From Walt Disney's "THE MICKEY MOUSE CLUB")

Bb TRUMPET

Words and Music by JIMMIE DODD
Arranged by MICHAEL SWEENEY

00860128

POWER ROCK
(We Will Rock You • Another One Bites The Dust)

B♭ TRUMPET

Moderate Rock

"We Will Rock You"

Arranged by MICHAEL SWEENEY

"Another One Bites The Dust"

WHEN THE SAINTS GO MARCHING IN

Words by KATHERINE E. PURVIS
Music by JAMES M. BLACK
Arranged by JOHN HIGGINS

B♭ TRUMPET

00860128

FARANDOLE
(From "L'Arlésienne")

Bb TRUMPET

GEORGES BIZET
Arranged by MICHAEL SWEENEY (ASCAP)

00860128

JUS' PLAIN BLUES

Bb TRUMPET

MICHAEL SWEENEY (ASCAP)

From the Paramount and Twentieth Century Fox Motion Picture TITANIC

MY HEART WILL GO ON

(Love Theme From 'Titanic')

Music by JAMES HORNER
Lyric by WILL JENNINGS
Arranged by PAUL LAVENDER

B♭ TRUMPET

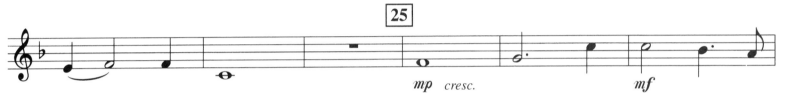

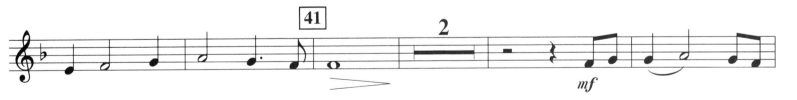

00860128

From THE MUPPET MOVIE

THE RAINBOW CONNECTION

Words and Music by PAUL WILLIAMS
and KENNITH L. ASCHER
Arranged by PAUL LAVENDER

B♭ TRUMPET

From Walt Disney's MARY POPPINS

SUPERCALIFRAGILISTICEXPIALIDOCIOUS

Words and Music by
RICHARD M. SHERMAN and ROBERT B. SHERMAN
Arranged by MICHAEL SWEENEY

B♭ TRUMPET

00860128

(From "THE SOUND OF MUSIC")

DO-RE-MI

Bb TRUMPET

Lyrics by **OSCAR HAMMERSTEIN II**
Music by **RICHARD RODGERS**
Arranged by PAUL LAVENDER

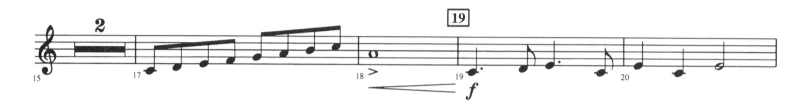

DRUMS OF CORONA

Bb TRUMPET

MICHAEL SWEENEY (ASCAP)

00860128

LAREDO
(Concert March)

Bb TRUMPET

JOHN HIGGINS

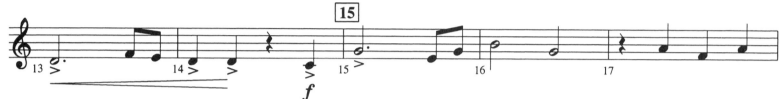

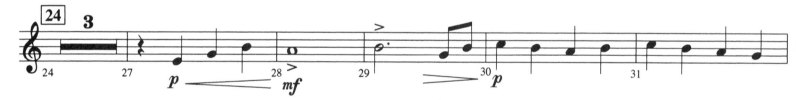

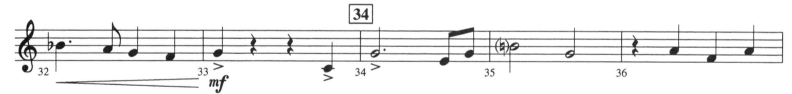

00860128

POMP AND CIRCUMSTANCE
March No. 1

By EDWARD ELGAR
Arranged by MICHAEL SWEENEY

Bb TRUMPET

00860128

STRATFORD MARCH

Bb TRUMPET

JOHN HIGGINS (ASCAP)